Biographies of famous people to
support the curriculum.

Francis
Drake

by Emma Fischel

Illustrations by Martin Remphry

Sch

W
FRANKLIN WATTS
LONDON • SYDNEY

First Published in 2000
by Franklin Watts
This edition 2001

Franklin Watts
96 Leonard Street
London EC2A 4XD

Franklin Watts Australia
56 O'Riordan Street
Alexandria, Sydney
NSW 2015

© 2000 text Emma Fischel
© 2000 illustrations Martin Remphry

The right of the author to be identified as the
author of this work has been asserted.

The right of the illustrator to be identified as
the illustrator of this work has been asserted.

ISBN 0 7496 4318 8

A CIP catalogue record for this book is
available from the British Library

Dewey Decimal Classification
Number:942.05

10 9 8 7 6 5 4 3 2 1

Series Editor: Sarah Ridley

Printed in Great Britain

Francis Drake

"It's a fine strong boy!" said Mr
and Mrs Drake proudly. "And
our first!"

Francis wasn't their last, though.
In the end he had eleven brothers.
But none of them became as
famous as baby Francis.

Things were very different in 1540. There were no fast cars, and no trains or planes to travel around in. Sailing ships were slow, and people knew much less about the world they lived in.

Most men and women hardly ever left their towns and villages.

The sea's got a big sharp edge and boats just fall off it!

Only a few brave explorers roamed the fierce and unknown seas in search of new lands and adventure.

Little did Francis know that he would grow up to become one of those adventurers.

God and religion were important to most people then, and Francis's father was a **VERY** religious man.

But there was a big argument going on between the two main religious groups in England.

When Francis was eight the Catholics burnt down his home. He and his family had to flee for their lives.

The Drakes' new home leaked and creaked. It floated ... just.

Francis didn't mind. It was right by a dockyard and, while his father preached to the sailors, Francis learnt about boats.

Children often went to work very young then. When Francis was only twelve, he started work on board ship.

"The sea is a dangerous place!" said the captain of the boat. "Mistakes mean death, so learn your lessons well!"

So Francis did.

He learnt about the fierce tides and currents, about hidden rocks that could tear boats apart.

He learnt by day and by night, in all kinds of weather.

Now Francis was eighteen and a new queen, Elizabeth I, was on the throne. She wanted to make England rich and strong.

Over in Spain, Philip II was busy making his country the richest and most powerful in Europe.

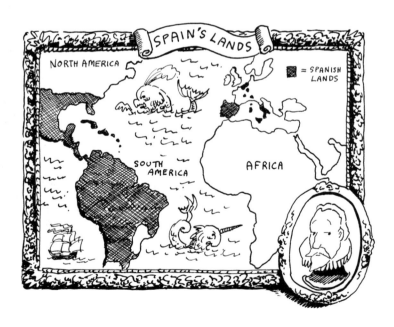

Some of Spain's newly discovered
lands were rich in treasures.
English ships braved storms and
death to travel there. Some came
home laden with gold and silver,
jewels and silks.

Francis longed to work on one of
those ships.

At last Francis's chance came.

"Join me!" said John Hawkins, captain of a small fleet of ships. "We sail to trade with the Spanish across the ocean!"

He shall captain a ship on the next trip.

For the next three years, Francis did just that.

But when Francis was twenty-five a terrible thing happened.

The Spanish invited the English to sail their fleet into harbour for peaceful trading ...

then they attacked.

Damn the Spanish! All those men and ships lost.

"Revenge!" Francis said. "From now on the Spanish are my enemy, on land or sea!"

He attacked a treasury nearby, where they kept huge amounts of Spanish gold. He seized it all.

And that was just the start.

No Spanish ship was safe from him. Time after time, Francis sailed home in ships laden with treasure.

And that made him a very important friend indeed ...

Shsh! Don't tell the Spanish I'm backing you.

From the Queen, To Francis Drake. Permission to loot and plunder Spanish Ships. 1572.

While Francis was away he had seen a vast ocean no Englishman had ever sailed before.

"Magellan of Portugal has sailed it," Francis said to the Queen. "Now let me do the same for England!"

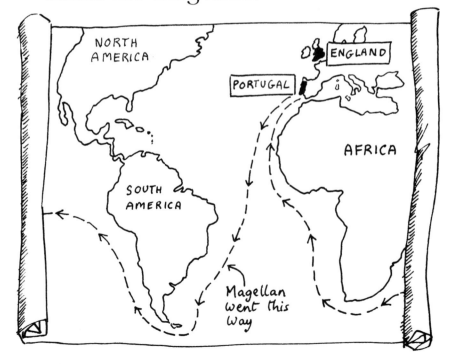

NORTH AMERICA

ENGLAND

PORTUGAL

AFRICA

SOUTH AMERICA

Magellan went this way

Now we know where every place in the world is. But back then there were still huge areas that no one had been to.

"Go!" said the Queen to Francis. "Find new lands, new routes, new places to trade. Make England rich!"

And bring back lots of lovely gold.

MAPS
MAPS

It was a cold December day when Francis set out.

Boats were terrible places below decks. They were dark, damp, squashed and smelly. The food was often mouldy and dirty.

Sometimes sailors would mutiny, and try to take over from the captain. Even Francis, a good captain, knew he had to be strict.

This man won't mutiny again. Anyone else like to try?

Francis took on board fresh food and water where he could along the coast.

Then terrifying storms struck. Huge waves and howling winds battered the little ships.

Days turned into weeks and still the storms raged on. Of the five ships that had set off, four sank or had to turn back for land.

Now Francis's ship sailed on alone into the vast Pacific Ocean.

There were no maps to show
Francis the shape and size of the
Pacific Ocean. He didn't know
where land was or where fierce
tides or rocks might be.

Sometimes he thought it was
the end.

SHIP'S LOG
68 days in this
small boat on a
huge unknown
sea. Will we starve
before we find
land?

At last, almost three years after Francis had first set out, he arrived home.

He was the first Englishman ever to have sailed right round the world!

THE GOLDEN HIND

PLYMOUTH

25

Francis hadn't forgotten his old enemy, Spain, while he was away. He had seized Spanish ships and treasure wherever he could.

Now his name struck fear and loathing into Spanish hearts.

In fact, they gave him a name, El Draque, meaning 'the dragon'.

The Dragon is here! Run for your lives!

"Return our treasures and off with his head!" thundered the Spanish.

In England Francis was a hero!

The Queen even came to visit him on his boat, and she had something to say to him.

Arise, Sir Francis Drake!

But over the next five years the Spanish king, Philip, grew more and more angry with Queen Elizabeth.

Things I don't like about the Queen of England:-
1. She's English.
2. She's the Queen.
3. She's not Catholic.
4. She helps Protestant rebels in countries I rule.
5. She backs pirates like Francis Drake.
6. She's sneaky.

In the end he decided what to do. "We shall arrest all English ships in our ports!" he said.

"Set sail, there's work to do!" said Francis when he heard the news. And so began another year of terror for the Spanish.

Now Philip was planning war against England. He began to gather together a huge fleet of ships, called the Armada.

Francis did all he could to stop him. In a Spanish port called Cadiz he sank or burned more than thirty Spanish ships.

He stormed a castle. He seized
ships on their way to join the
Armada. He captured gold the
Spanish needed to pay for war.

But even Francis could only
slow things down.

Back home, Francis found some people still saying the Queen should work for peace.

"Peace will never come," Francis said to them. "But Spanish galleons will – and soon! We must prepare to fight!"

My Lord Walsingham,
I dare almost not
write of the great
forces we hear the
King of Spain has.
Prepare in England
strongly,

and most by
sea!

He wrote to everyone important
he could and, at last, England
began to prepare for war.

Francis was made a
Vice-Admiral in the navy,
in charge of a big group of ships.

Admiral Howard,
I shall serve
you well.

Impatient young
hothead! We can't
have him in charge.

News came of the first sighting
of the Armada while Francis was
playing a game called boules.

"A huge fleet of Spanish
galleons are on their way,"
gasped the messenger.
"It will soon be here!"

"There is plenty of time to finish the game and beat the Spanish too!" Francis said.

Beacons were lit on hilltops all along the land. And that night, Francis and his fleet set sail to do battle with the mighty Armada.

"Certain death lies ahead!"
cried the English sailors. "We
cannot defeat these huge ships!"

"Courage!" said Francis. "Our
ships are small but fast and
nimble. We know the waters
and the winds. This is *our* sea!"

The first shot was fired. The battle began.

Soon Francis captured one of the most important Spanish ships. He found out a lot about the Spanish battle plans.

"Attack from the sides!" said Francis. "Shoot to stop them getting too close! Twist and turn, use the tides and the winds to keep them out at sea. Force them away from our coast!"

"What can we do?" said the Spanish soldiers. "They're too well armed! They won't let us near enough to fight. They won't let us land. Our ships are too big to move quickly!"

There were three battles at sea. Slowly the English forced the Spanish across the sea to France.

"Let's set eight of our oldest ships alight!" said Francis and the other leaders. "The wind will blow them into the Spanish fleet. Who knows, eight ships lost may mean a war won!"

And, in the dead of night, that's exactly what they did.

"Flee!" cried the Spanish.

"After them!" cried Francis, and the English fleet chased them up the coast, fighting all the way.

In less than a month it was over.
What was left of the Armada,
the greatest war fleet ever to
threaten England, was gone.

And, except for the eight old ships set alight, not one English ship had been lost in the whole battle.

Francis lived for another eight years. He died while at sea — and was buried there too.

Further facts

More about Francis

Francis married twice, but had no children. His second wife, Elizabeth Sydenham, was very rich and they lived in a huge house in Devon.

After the Armada, Francis became mayor of Plymouth, then a member of parliament. He did make other expeditions after the Armada, but nothing as successful as earlier ones.

Chatham Chest

Francis, together with John Hawkins, set up something called the Chatham Chest. It gave money and help to sick sailors. Many sailors were treated

very badly when they got back from the Armada. Some of them even died on the streets.

Francis's drum

Francis had a drum which he took with him on his voyages. You can still see it in Buckland Abbey in Devon. Legend says that whenever England faces danger the beat of his drum will summon Francis to her defence.

Some important dates in Sir Francis Drake's lifetime

1540   Francis is born in Tavistock, Devon.

1549   Francis and his family are driven out of their home.

1558   Elizabeth I becomes Queen of England.

1565   Francis sets sail on his first expedition with John Hawkins.

1568   The Spanish betray Francis at San Juan de Ulua.

1573   Francis sees the Pacific for the first time.

1577   Francis sets out to sail across the Pacific and around the world.

1580   Francis arrives home and is knighted.

1587   Francis destroys 33 enemy ships in Cadiz harbour.

1588   The Spanish Armada is defeated.

1593   Francis becomes a member of parliament.

1596   Francis dies at sea.